R.E.I. Editions

All of our ebooks can be read on the following devices:
- Computers
- eReaders
- iOS
- Android
- Blackberries
- Windows
- Tablet
- Cell phone

French Academy

Ajna

The Sixth Chakra

ISBN: 978-2-37297-4806

Publication: January 2013

Work plan

1- Muladhara - The First Chakra

2 - Svadhishtana - The Second Chakra

3 - Manipura - The Third Chakra

4 - Anahata - The Fourth Chakra

5 - Vishuddha - The Fifth Chakra

6 - Ajna - The Sixth Chakra

7 - Sahasrara - The Seventh Chakra

French Academy

Ajna
The Sixth Chakra

R.E.I. Editions

Book Index

The chakra system

The word Chakra, which comes from Sanskrit and means "wheel", is meant to indicate the seven basic energy centers in the human body. Chakras are centers of subtle psychic energy located along the spine. Each of these centers is connected, at the level of subtle energies, to the main ganglia of the nerves which branch off from the vertebral column. In addition, the chakras are related to the levels of consciousness, to the archetypal elements, to the phases inherent in the development of life, to the colors, which are closely linked to the chakras, because they are found outside our body, but inside the aura , or the electromagnetic field that surrounds each person, to sounds, body functions and much, much more. The Eastern doctrine that has spread knowledge of them in the Western world considers the Chakras as openings, gateways to the essence of the human body. The chakras are usually represented inside a lotus flower, with a variable number of open petals. The open petals represent the chakra in its full opening. On each petal is written one of the fifty letters of the Sanskrit alphabet, which are considered sacred letters, therefore, divine expression. Furthermore, each of them expresses a different activity of the human being, a different state, both manifest and still potential. Each chakra resonates on a different frequency which corresponds to the colors of the rainbow.

The seven main Chakras also correspond to the seven main glands of our endocrine system. Their main function is to absorb the Universal Energy, metabolize it, break it down and convey it along the energy channels up to the nervous system, feed the auras and release energy outside. Most everyone sees them as funnels, simultaneously swirling and flowing energy back and forth. Each of the seven centers has both an anterior (usually dominant) component and a posterior (usually less dominant) component, which are intimately connected, with the exception, however, of the first and seventh, which, however, are single.

From the second to the fifth, the anterior aspect relates to feelings and emotions, while the posterior aspect relates to the will. As regards the anterior and posterior sixth, and the seventh, the correlation is with the mind and reason. The first and seventh. they also have the very important connection function for the human being: being the most external Chakras of the energy channel, they have the characteristic of placing man in relation with the Universe on one side and with the Earth on the other. The perfect functioning of the energy system is synonymous with good health. There are many techniques to open the Chakras, including Reiki, which stands out for its peculiar sweetness and for the possibility of harmonizing any energy imbalances.

Each center oversees certain organs, and has particular functions on an emotional, psychic and spiritual level. Among the seven fundamental ones, there are precise affinities.

- The First with the Seventh: Basic Energy with Spirit Energy.
- The Second with the Sixth: Energy of feeling on a material level with Energy of feeling on an extrasensory level.
- The Third with the Fifth: Energy of the working mind and personal power with Energy of the higher mind and communication.
- The Fourth: bridge between the upper three and the lower three and alchemical forge of transformation.

Each Chakra is associated with a color, which corresponds to and derives from the frequency and vibration of the center itself. Furthermore, each Chakra corresponds to a mantra, the sound of a musical note and, in some cases, even a natural element, a planet or a zodiac sign. Because the chakra system is the primary processing center for every function of our being, blockage or energetic insufficiency in the chakras usually causes unrest in body, mind, or spirit. A defect in the flow of energy through a given chakra will cause a defect in the energy supplied to the connected parts of the physical body, as well as affect all levels of being. This is because an energy field is a Holistic entity; every part of it affects every other part. Essential oils are able to tune into specific chakras: their scent and their vibration gently put us in deep contact with our energy centers.

The massage with specific essential oils on the points corresponding to the chakras activates and balances their action, harmonizing and strengthening the entire body. Starting from the bottom they are:

- 1st = Muladhara
- 2nd = Swadhisthana
- 3rd = Manipura
- 4th = Anahata
- 5th = Vhishuddhi
- 6th = Ajna
- 7th = Sahasrara

Furthermore, each of the seven chakras comes to represent an important area of human psychic health, which we can briefly summarize as:

1. Survival
2. Sexuality
3. Strength
4. Love
5. Communication
6. Intuition
7. Cognition.

Metaphorically the chakras are related to the following archetypal elements:

1. Earth
2. Water
3. Fire
4. Air
5. Sound
6. Light
7. Thought

Ajna - The Sixth Chakra

The sixth chakra is the brow chakra, "the third eye."
It has two indigo lotus petals as its symbol and is placed in the center of the forehead, about two fingers above the root of the nose, in the position of the third eye. Its name in Sanskrit means to know, to perceive and also to command.
It is the last chakra located within the physical body. On the two petals of the lotus are the letters Ham and Ksam.
The sixth is the chakra of superior mental structure and superior vision, commonly called the third eye, considered fundamental in many oriental meditative practices (Tibet and India above all). It develops in adulthood.
It expresses the right to see the truth, be it human or superior. It presides over the sense of sight.
In its anterior expression it is associated with the faculty of visualizing and making intellectual concepts comprehensible and, in its posterior expression, with the faculty of implementing the concepts themselves. If the sixth chakra is not harmonious, the person will easily find himself in a situation of confusion in which ideas and concepts will correspond to reality and consequently his actions, i.e. his ability to translate ideas into practice will fall or worse still, distorted ideas and concepts will be brought forward with the appropriate consequences for oneself and for others.

Perception, knowledge and command are the prerogatives of this chakra.

It lets you enter the non-material world, the invisible, through extrasensory perception to bring knowledge and, therefore, deep awareness of what surrounds the human being, not only in matter and consequently allowing to command and guide your own existence.

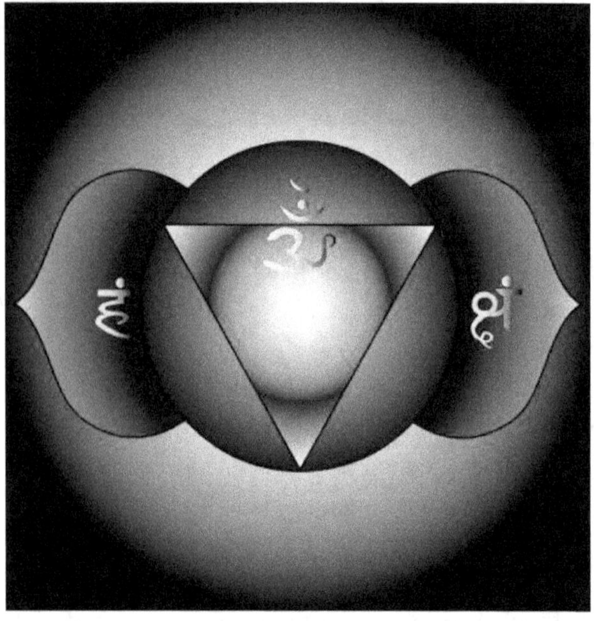

Speaking of this chakra, esoteric practice suggests that the spiritually highest Tibetan monks (lamas) undergo the surgical opening of the sixth chakra which allows them, not only to expand their consciousness, but also to connect with each other telepathically .

They are also able to immediately and clearly recognize any negativity, as well as the spiritual potential of the human beings they encounter. This center in the physical body is represented by the crossing of the two optic nerves in our brain (the "chiasm optic") and would control the functioning of the pituitary gland and the eyes. Excessive eyestrain (from cinema, television, computers or reading books) would harm this chakra which would also be damaged by bad thoughts.

This chakra would allow us to think about the future, create projects, develop extrasensory perceptions such as the ability to see without the use of the sense of sight, to reach mystical states, to perceive the so-called aura (a presumed field that would surround people, unknown to science, not to be confused with what is called aura in medicine) and to travel in the so-called "astral plane". The chakra would close in case of disappointments due to the failure to carry out a life project. The imbalances would manifest themselves through nightmares, uncontrolled or unpleasant psychic phenomena, complete lack of dreams, mental confusion and with diseases related to vision and frontal headaches.

The sixth Chakra represents thinking, it is also called the Third Eye Chakra. This is the seat of the highest mental faculties, intellectual abilities, as well as memory and will. By developing our awareness, and opening the third eye more and more, our imagination will be able to produce the energy necessary to realize our desires.

When the Heart Chakra is open and in conjunction with the Third Eye Chakra, we can transmit our healing energies both from near and far. At the same time we can have access to all levels of creation, levels that go beyond even physical reality. Knowledge of this kind comes to us in the form of intuition, clairvoyance, and hypersensitivity to hearing and perceiving. Things that we had only vaguely suspected before now appear clearly to us. This chakra rules dreams.

There are three types of dreams:

- Unconscious dreams, which bring up old issues from the subconscious so that we can gain a clearer understanding of how we really feel, rather than how we "should" feel. We may perceive these dreams as nightmares or as opportunities to be aware of our own darkness so it can be healed and released.
- Conscious dreams, which are often "dress rehearsals" for what we are doing and trying to do in day life. After having these dreams we may feel tired, as if we have worked all night and, in a sense, we have.
- Superconscious dreams, which allow us to make real waking journeys through the inner planes. It is important to write down these dreams and integrate them into everyday life, as they are a true spiritual guide.

Even if a dream is not remembered, it still releases psychic tension. Research has shown that people who have received adequate sleep but have been deprived of

dreams become disoriented and psychologically disturbed. It is even more beneficial if we learn to remember important dreams, because they give us important information about our Self.
There are two effective ways to remember dreams.
- One: we say to ourselves, before falling asleep: "I will remember my dreams".
- Two: before we open our eyes in the morning, we tell ourselves what our dream was.

This activity transfers dreams from the right cerebral hemisphere, the one that imagines, to the language areas of the left cerebral hemisphere. Then, often, we can remember the dreams long enough to write them down. Some dreams are not difficult to remember and, in fact, haunt us until we process them to a full understanding of their meaning.
The consciousness of this chakra opens and drops the "veil of maya", the illusion of worldly appearances. It would also represent the power to see-know what hasn't happened yet, but is about to happen. In the sector identified by this chakra are the diencephalon and two glands of fundamental importance for the control and regulation of the whole organism, the pituitary and the epiphysis, i.e. the pituitary and pineal glands.
Both manifest within our body as our ego and superego.
The pituitary gland hangs approximately in the center of the lower part of the emphalus, below the third ventricle, and is housed in a niche of the sphenoid bone called, due to its shape, the sella turcica.

It is composed of two fundamental parts, of ectodermal derivation: the neuro-hypophysis, derived from the floor of the diencephalon (it contains a recess of the third ventricle), and the adeno-hypolysis, derived from the vault of the stomodeum, i.e. from the primitive buccal cavity. In some animal species, as evidence of this derivation and of the primitive site of elimination of the pituitary secretion, a communication duct remains between the pituitary and the buccal cavity (in some fish; in some reptiles and birds only a closed cord remains).

These ancestral ways of communication between compartments of the body, which appear completely separate in humans, force us to reflect on the words of yogis who claim they can reactivate normally closed paths and communications within the body. The hormones of the pituitary gland are STH-growth hormone; TSH-thyroid stimulating hormone; ACTH-hormone that stimulates the adrenocortical; FSH-hormone that stimulates the growth of the ovarian follicle; LH-hormone that stimulates the corpus luteum (interstitial cells in males); PRL-hormone that stimulates lactation. The hormone of the middle part is the melanocyte-stimulating hormone MSH (regulates skin pigmentation).

The neuro-hypophysis does not synthesize hormones, but accumulates and releases the neuro-secretions accumulated by the hypothalamus; the most important are oxytocin, which stimulates uterine contractions and the release of milk from the breast, and vasopressin, which stimulates the reabsorption of water in the kidney.

As you can see, the pituitary controls the whole body, because it controls the endocrine glands. What happens in the diencephalon-pituitary system therefore prefigures the bodily or psychic modifications that will manifest themselves in the individual. A dysfunction of this system will therefore lead to an imbalance in all the psycho-physical functions of the individual. Observing the role of the pituitary gland in the body we can say, using a figurative language but relevant to reality, that this gland (or rather, the diencephalon-pituitary system) represents "the established order", the "royalty" that governs, the ability to prefigure, project, integrate, control all the functions of the body, or, for yoga, what exists in the «microcosm».

The epiphysis is a small pine cone-shaped gland less than 1 cm long and weighing 150 grams, located at the level of the posterior wall of the third ventricle, to which it is connected by a peduncle, such as the pituitary. Going up the evolutionary ladder, above the amphibians the pineal becomes essentially glandular, although still little known sensory cells remain, and the main hormone it produces is melatonin which is rhythmically secreted following the light-dark cycles of the external environment, even if the gland is no longer in direct contact with the external source of light (for example, in humans). It is as if his visual function, previously direct, had been able to internalize itself. In fact, the pineal receives an afferent innervation from the superior cervical ganglion of the sympathetic, which in turn is connected to the eye. The perception of darkness causes melatonin synthesis which, by inducing the aggregation of melanin granules in the skin, lightens the skin.

Light, on the other hand, decreases sympathetic nerve impulses and blocks hormone synthesis: a few minutes of exposure to bright light are enough to cause a drop in circulating levels of melatonin. The integrity of this pathway is essential for the activity of the gland.

Following the light-dark rhythms, the epiphysis in fact synchronizes and synchronizes the whole organism on the rhythms of day and night, of the seasons, etc., that is, on the rhythms of the macrocosm that surrounds it.

The epiphysis would therefore be an internal-external "synchronizer", a guide of the temporal structure of the organism: regardless of the vision, the organism knows if it is day or night or in which period of the year we are.

At the same time, the epiphysis dictates the rhythm of the internal "seasons": melatonin decreases in puberty, during ovulation, in menopause, in old age. All this through a transformation of the light impulse which, materializing, becomes a hormonal impulse. Light, nerve impulse, epiphysis, hormone: the coagulating function of Saturn of the alchemists, the third eye of the Orient. At the current state of research, epiphyseal biorhythms seem to control mood, hormonal balance, immune balance and appear to have an anti-stress action. In summary, the organic functions corresponding to this chakra are control over the balance of the entire psycho-soma, control of the capacity for self-recognition or maintenance of the integrity of one's individuality, the internalization of visual abilities previously directed towards the outside, with greater possibility of self-regulation and self-synchronization. As always, we find a correspondence between the symbolism of the chakra and the functions of the organs included in its wheel.

If the functions are these, it is even more understandable how the opening of this chakra allows one to have consciousness and control over the entire human microcosm, to lift the veil of maya, the illusions, freeing the individual from the "spectre of the dragon uroboric», that is, total unconsciousness, which always tries to reabsorb it into itself.

How to activate the 6th chakra

- Take regular night walks, look at the starry sky and feel the calm, peace and strength of the night.
- Revive your imagination, especially by reading complex novels and fairy tales.
- Wear indigo or purple clothing, or decorate your home in the same color.
- Be interested in the teachings of Eastern and Western wisdom, write down your dreams in a diary, in this way they will become more intense and will strengthen your imagination and intuition.
- The voice "I" stimulates this chakra, and we will use it, as usual, vibrating it while we breathe sitting on the floor.
- Essential oils: violet, lemongrass and cajeput stimulate this chakra. Choose one and put 3 or 4 drops in an essence diffuser or in your bath water, after having diluted them with a little milk.
- Gemstones: the following gemstones strengthen the ajna chakra: amethyst, blue sapphire, opal, blue tourmaline, sodalite, lapis lazuli.

Color of the sixth chakra

The color associated with the 6th chakra is indigo.
Indigo is a color that has always been considered very particular as it is the meeting point between blue and violet and is, contrary to the other colors of the spectrum, more of a nuance than a real dye. Indigo is a powerful color and should be used sparingly. Its characteristics are similar to those of blue, but with a deeper effect, also due to its higher gradation and frequency. It is a symbol of spirituality, it represents the relationship with our inner abilities. Indigo influences our senses by improving mood in case of melancholy or light depressive states. Furthermore, the indigo color has a strong relaxing power and helps in meditative practices. This color acts positively on everything concerning the central nervous system and on all five senses. So it helps to significantly improve sight, hearing, touch, smell and taste. It acts on two glands that are important to us: the pituitary gland (pituitary gland, which regulates hormones and the metabolic activity of the whole body) and the pineal gland (epiphysis, which regulates the production of melatonin and the sleep-wake cycle). Anyone who loves indigo is a reserved, sensitive and imaginative person, internally rich, characterized by a dual inclination: on the one hand, he tends to isolate himself from the world, as a consequence of a critical judgment on the baseness of everyday reality, but on the other, in at the same time,

he aspires to a communion of souls, out of a desire to find like-minded people. Indigo can be defined as the color of knowledge, balance, purification. It is a color that enhances spirituality, but it is inadvisable, like all "cold" colors, for those who experience moments of fear or depression. People who cannot harmonize with the world around them dislike the color indigo.

In Ayurvedic medicine it is used as an antidote to cobra venom. Indigo is also a color with strong thermal insulating properties; it is no coincidence that the Tuaregs use tunics dyed with this color to better withstand the desert temperatures.

- Indigo is so relaxing that it is used as a pain reliever, be it physical or spiritual.
- It is good to use it in the meditation phase, when we are afflicted by problems and worries, when we seem to have to face an insurmountable difficulty.
- Indigo is the color of solutions, because it helps to open the mind. It has a strong soothing power.

Indigo is a color of harmony that can be used at any time of the day, according to one's feelings. It is advisable to take a bath a day for at least 7 consecutive days, this to allow the body to recharge the energy of the colour, then reduce the use to 2/3 baths a week, according to one's needs.

The sixth chakra is the brow chakra, third eye. It has two indigo lotus petals as its symbol and is placed in the center of the forehead, about two fingers above the root of the nose, in the position of the third eye. Its name in

Sanskrit means to know, to perceive and also to command. It is the last chakra located within the physical body. On the two petals of the lotus are the letters Ham and Ksam. The sixth is the chakra of superior mental structure and superior vision, commonly called the third eye, considered fundamental in many oriental meditative practices (Tibet and India above all). It develops in adulthood. It expresses the right to see the truth, be it human or superior. It presides over the sense of sight.

In its anterior expression it is associated with the faculty of visualizing and making intellectual concepts comprehensible and, in its posterior expression, with the faculty of implementing the concepts themselves. If the sixth chakra is not harmonious, the person will easily find himself in a situation of confusion in which ideas and concepts will correspond to reality and consequently his actions, i.e. his ability to translate ideas into practice will fall or worse still, distorted ideas and concepts will be brought forward with the appropriate consequences for oneself and for others. Perception, knowledge and command are the prerogatives of this chakra. It lets you enter the non-material world, the invisible, through extrasensory perception to bring knowledge and, therefore, deep awareness of what surrounds the human being, not only in matter and consequently allowing to command and guide your own existence.

Speaking of this chakra, esoteric practice suggests that the spiritually highest Tibetan monks (lamas) undergo the surgical opening of the sixth chakra which allows them, not only to expand their consciousness, but also to connect with each other telepathically . They are also able to immediately and clearly recognize any negativity, as well as the spiritual potential, of the human beings they encounter. This center in the physical body is represented by the crossing of the two optic nerves in our brain (the "chiasm optic") and would control the functioning of the pituitary gland and the eyes. Excessive eyestrain (from cinema, television, computers or reading books) would harm this chakra which would also be damaged by bad thoughts.

This chakra would allow us to think about the future, create projects, develop extrasensory perceptions such as the ability to see without the use of the sense of sight, to reach mystical states, to perceive the so-called aura (a presumed field that would surround people, unknown to science, not to be confused with what is called aura in medicine) and to travel in the so-called "astral plane". The chakra would close in case of disappointments due to the failure to carry out a life project. The imbalances would manifest themselves through nightmares, uncontrolled or unpleasant psychic phenomena, complete lack of dreams, mental confusion and with diseases related to vision and frontal headaches. The sixth Chakra represents thinking, it is also called the Third Eye Chakra. This is the seat of the highest mental faculties, intellectual abilities, as well as memory and will. By developing our awareness, and opening the third eye more and more, our imagination will be able to produce the energy necessary to realize our desires. When the Heart Chakra is open and in conjunction with the Third Eye Chakra, we can transmit our healing energies both from near and far. At the same time we can have access to all levels of creation, levels that go beyond even physical reality. Knowledge of this kind comes to us in the form of intuition, clairvoyance, and hypersensitivity to hearing and perceiving. Things that we had only vaguely suspected before now appear clearly to us.

As always, we find a correspondence between the symbolism of the chakra and the functions of the organs included in its wheel. If the functions are these, it is even more understandable how the opening of this chakra allows one to have consciousness and control over the entire human microcosm, to lift the veil of maya, the illusions, freeing the individual from the "spectre of the dragon uroboric», that is, total unconsciousness, which always tries to reabsorb it into itself.

- If indigo is in excess there will be moments of distraction, you may be led to daydreaming, barred in action, with fantastical fixations and beliefs. The excess of indigo energy could therefore cause episodes of hallucination, illusions, obsessions, nightmares.
- If the indigo will be in defect you will be numb, with poor memory and poor imagination, visualization difficulties, inability to remember dreams, tendency to deny the evidence. The lack of indigo energy would cause vision problems, skin alterations often on an emotional basis, tears easily.

- Indications:
- It is a purifier of the circulatory system, including the blood, and also a mental purifier.
- It is useful for eye inflammation, ear and hearing diseases.
- By projecting an indigo-colored ray into the ear of those suffering from tinnitus (ringing or ear sounds), the pathology can be eradicated.
- In fevers associated with dysfunctions of the lymphatic system, it is radiated to the groin and under the armpits.
- Many sportsmen adopt it to tone up the muscle, as indigo purifies the blood and improves the tissues, even on the surface.
- Promotes the production of phagocytes in the spleen.
- Contraindications:
- Individuals who tend to take charge of everyone's problems.
- Introspective people who often suffer from anxiety attacks or nightmares.
- Depression.

Essential oils associated with the sixth chakra

Mint, myrrh, violet, lemongrass, cajeput, anise, helichrysum, sage, angelica and lavender activate the fifth chakra.

Mix each individual essential oil with a carrier oil, such as jojoba or almond oil, in the ratio of 2 drops per tablespoon of carrier oil, then 2 drops per 10 mL of carrier. Since this is a "vibrational treatment", a very diluted mixture will have a deeper and more marked action. Massage the chakra you want to work on with the blend containing the chosen essential oil. Use a few drops and apply them slowly with your fingertips and in a clockwise circular motion. While massaging the Chakra, focus on the result you want to achieve, visualizing the harmonic energy of the oil as it opens and rebalances the chakra. After the treatment, lie down and relax for a while, allowing the Chakra to rebalance itself. Breathe deeply and slowly, trying to clear and empty your mind as much as possible.

As an alternative to the massage, add a few drops of the essential oil chosen for the treatment to the essence diffuser. Concentrate and focus on your therapeutic intention, visualize the aromatherapy energy of the essential oil, open and rebalance the chakra.

Relax for at least half an hour.

Mint

The name "mint" comes from the Greek Mintha, a nymph daughter of Cocito, one of the five rivers of the Underworld, loved by Pluto and transformed into a plant by the goddess Persephone, his wife.

According to mythology, the goddess discovered her husband's betrayal and, seized by a fit of jealousy, wanted to take revenge on her by transforming her into an inconspicuous and apparently insignificant plant, relegating her to grow near the banks of her father's river, near the waters . However, in order not to completely disdain Pluto, he allowed the seedling to still possess something pleasant in every part of her body: the fresh aroma of her perfume.

Pliny already enumerated all its properties, exalting its fragrance, "able to excite the soul and stimulate the appetite".

Mint-based preparations, according to the Roman historian, cured tonsillar angina, blood spitting from tuberculosis, hiccups, vomiting, and helped eliminate parasites. In the 18th century Nicolò Lemery, in his Treatise on Simple Drugs, set out his interpretation of the presumed exciting and tonic virtues of the plant: "Mentha is dedicated to the mind because this plant, by fortifying the brain, awakens thoughts or memory".

When inhaled, it has a refreshing and rejuvenating effect on the psyche.

It is effectively used to promote concentration during study for exams, or to improve performance in the office. Peppermint essential oil also has a toning action, useful in case of psycho-physical fatigue and neuro-vegetative problems, due to states of stress, such as anxiety, insomnia, depression.

• Invigorating

If massaged locally it is useful for all types of headaches, from digestive ones to those coming from pressure changes. Also excellent for relieving neck tension, menstrual pain, sprains, muscle pain and rheumatism as it has an analgesic and anti-rheumatic action. Two drops of mint in a spoonful of almond oil and massage locally for persistent cramps, bad digestion; on the temples in case of headache.

• Environmental diffusion

1 drop of mint essential oil, for each square meter of the environment in which it spreads, by means of an essential oil burner or in the water of radiator humidifiers, for a regenerating and purifying effect in smokers' rooms and in the rooms of those who study.

• Contraindications

Do not apply pure peppermint essential oil to the skin, but always mix it with a base oil (jojoba oil, sweet almond oil).

It is not suitable for children under the age of 12.
It is advisable that those who follow a homeopathic cure avoid the use of peppermint essential oil, because interactions could occur. Pay attention to the eyes, as it is highly irritating to the mucous membranes. Do not exceed the recommended dose.

Myrrh

It belongs to the resin family and, in fact, is associated with incense and gold, recalling the legend of the Magi and the gifts they brought to Jesus after his birth. The supply difficulties and the commercial hoarding made it, in fact, a precious gift. The ancient history books mention it up to more than 3,000 years ago. It has been used for centuries as a component of incense for religious purposes.

The Egyptians used it, as well as in sun worship rites, also in embalming processes, in mixtures with other essential oils. In ancient Greece myrrh was widely used, up to mixing it with wine and a mythological episode tells of its origin, linking it to Myrrh, daughter of the king of Cyprus, who for having had incestuous relationships with her father, was transformed by Aphrodite into a tree from the scented resin. From this union after nine months the tree-woman gave birth to Adonis. Its astringent, disinfectant and healing properties have been known for centuries.

The ancients used to carry myrrh paste with them into battle to spread on wounds. Egyptian women used it in face masks against wrinkles, as they still do in Africa and Arab countries. Israelis put powdered myrrh directly on the toothbrush as toothpaste. In traditional Chinese medicine it is used as a healing remedy for sores and hemorrhoids and in menstrual cycle problems, such as amenorrhea.

Today it is present in almost all European national pharmacopoeias.

- Part used: resinoid.
- Extraction method: steam distillation.
- Base note: warm, spicy, bitter, balsamic scent.

- **Harmonizing**

This oil is highly valued in aromatherapy as a sedative, antidepressant and as a promoter of spiritual feelings. Myrrh serves to balance the spiritual world with the material one, giving us strength and optimism, especially helps people who are afraid to reveal their feelings. It makes us humble and devoted, preparing us to receive energy and love from others. It helps to overcome the fear of death and the pain of separation. Queen of emotional blocks and our inability to live spiritually, it stimulates us especially during sleep by eliminating all excesses in us.

- **Environmental diffusion**

1 drop of myrrh essential oil for every square meter of the environment in which it spreads, by means of an essential oil burner or in the water of radiator humidifiers, against coughs and colds and to disinfect the air of the rooms.

- **Cosmetic use**

Compresses against eczema: put 6-7 drops of myrrh in 300 ml of distilled water. With sterile gauze compresses, apply compresses to the affected areas. Repeat daily until you notice an improvement.

- **Contraindications**

Myrrh essential oil is non-irritating, does not cause sensitization and is non-toxic at low doses. Use sparingly. It is absolutely to be avoided its internal use during pregnancy and breastfeeding. Myrrh, in high doses, can cause sweating, nausea, vomiting and rapid heartbeat..

Violet

The essential oil is extracted from fresh flowers, which are collected during the period of maximum flowering, by steam distillation. The product obtained is a greenish liquid, which gives off a very intense aroma.
The scent of violet essential oil is considered an aphrodisiac. By adding the essential oils of violet, nutmeg and jasmine to the bath water, feminine sensitivity is stimulated and mind and body are relaxed.

- A refreshing compress based on violet essence soothes headaches, thanks to its astringent properties. Add 1 drop of essential oil to 1/4 liter of water and immerse a handkerchief in it, squeeze it and place it on the forehead. Then lie down for about half an hour and relax. If necessary, repeat the application.

the violet, sensitive and delicate, can be used where one wishes to increase sensitivity, receptivity, creativity of thought, to soothe wounds of existence and in particular the disappointments of love: in fact, it is believed that its perfume "comforts and invigorate the heart".
The aroma is exquisitely feminine, but it can be used, for massages or baths, also for the male sex, to soften and smooth the edges of a rough character, or for those who are too prosaic, alien to poetry and feeling to the extent of a drop to add to more masculine essences. In the amorous-sexual sphere, the violet acts at the level of the heart, in the sense that it sweetens, inclines to love

and sentiment, but thanks to the action of the "blue that mixes with red" and which adds a refreshing note, it brightens the mind and makes it more open, more reflective and calm, relaxes and lowers tensions.

- On an organic level, the violet has expectorant properties useful in case of cough or bronchitis, purifies the skin and cleanses the pores (in these cases it is indicated for washing or including hot water, steam baths); stimulates circulation and has an anti-inflammatory action in case of circulatory problems in the limbs or rheumatism.

Lemongrass

The precious essential oil, with an aroma very similar to that of lemon, is extracted from the fresh, slightly dried plant and has a yellowish color tending towards brown.
Citronella essential oil has stimulating properties, so much so that in aromatherapy it is used to ward off states of sadness and depression.
If spread on the body it has a detoxifying and relaxing action, fights hyper sweating and acts as a deodorant. It also dissolves fat from the surface of the skin, fighting acne and seborrhea, even on the scalp. Traditional Chinese medicine has used lemongrass as a remedy for rheumatism for centuries. Other populations use the active ingredients contained in its leaves to fight intestinal parasites, to ward off insects, against digestive problems and fever. Lemongrass has a lemon-like odor and is widely used in India and other Asian countries as an ingredient in sauces and soups and for preparing herbal teas.
As a stimulant, lemongrass essential oil exerts its stimulating activities on the nervous system:

- Generates a state of calm, relaxation and optimism, drives away the gloomy thoughts that dispose the soul to depression and sadness.
- Performs a positive action in case of headaches due to nervous tension, stress, psychophysical tiredness and states of deconcentration.

Used when driving for many hours, a few drops on a handkerchief stimulates the driver's attention. Like all essential oils, it has an antiseptic action on bacteria, especially those that cause bad smells. If diluted 2 drops in foot bath water it is effective against excessive sweating.

- **Massage**

For a relaxing massage, dilute 3 drops of lemongrass essential oil in 2 teaspoons of sweet almond oil. If massaged on the belly it is useful for those suffering from slow digestion, meteorism, or abdominal spasms; when applied to the forehead and temples, this mixture is indicated against headaches caused by nervous tension.
Internal use: thanks to its sedative properties, it produces a rapid calming effect. 2 or 3 drops diluted in a sugar cube or a teaspoon of honey, 1-2 times a day.

- **Contraindications**

In some individuals, allergies may occur when in contact with the leaves of the plant. Therefore, the use of pure essential oil on the skin is not recommended. Excessive and prolonged inhalation can increase the heart rate and is therefore not recommended for those suffering from tachycardia and palpitations.
To be avoided in pregnancy.

Cajeput

Cajeput essential oil is considered one of the most powerful natural antiseptics in existence. It has a calming and harmonizing effect on the body at the same time. In aromatherapy it constitutes a top note, due to its high volatility and rapidity of action.

- The antiseptic characteristics make it beneficial in the treatment of respiratory system disorders such as asthma, bronchitis, cough, sore throat and sinusitis. It is also used for the treatment of cystitis and prostatitis.

The various uses and the numerous beneficial properties allow it to be used in place of the better known Tea Tree essential oil, compared to which it has a less penetrating scent. Originally from Australia, the Philippines, Indonesia and Vietnam, cajeput is grown in Oceania, India and Florida. The name of the plant and of the oil come from the Malay kaju-puti, which means "white tree", due to the color of the wood. Clear colorless or yellow-green liquid. The coloring is due to the oxidation of the copper, transferred from the stills, or to the presence of colored vegetable substances such as chlorophyll. It has a special, grateful smell, which recalls that of camphor and rosemary, with a first acrid, burning and then refreshing and bitter, aromatic taste.

- As an analgesic, if massaged on painful parts it has an anti-inflammatory action, useful in the symptomatic treatment of headaches, joint pains, arthritis, neuralgia and gout.

In case of rheumatism or muscle pain, sweet almond oil will be a perfect base oil in which to dilute the essence. Add 250 ml of sweet almond oil to 25 drops of cajeput essential oil. Use this mixture twice a day to massage areas affected by rheumatic or muscle pain. The effect will be better if you cover the part with a warm woolen cloth.

- **Contraindications**

No contraindications are described for the use of this essential oil, although caution is advised in pregnant women. In high doses, cajeput essential oil can cause nausea, vomiting and gastritis. The assumption should not be made in the presence of known hypersensitivity to its components. It may enhance the effect or metabolism of drugs, including barbiturates and orally administered blood sugar lowering drugs..

Anise

Green aniseed fruits are used to aid digestion and eliminate gas present in the stomach and intestines, in the treatment of coughs, to thin bronchial secretions and aid in the expectoration of phlegm and as a galactogogue, i.e. to increase milky production.

Anise also has antispasmodic virtues against intestinal cramps and sedative in the case of insomnia and nervous excitement.

The Greeks used anise seeds to thin phlegm. In ancient times, the green anise plant was considered sacred for its medicinal properties. At the table of the Assyrian king Assurbanipal could not be missing for its digestive properties. To this end it was also introduced as a kind of subsistence in the baggage of the military also for the carminative and disinfectant properties of the gastrointestinal tract.

The monks introduced green anise in their recipes for making flavored liqueurs.

Contraindications: should not be used during pregnancy as it stimulates uterine contractions. In high doses, green anise essential oil can cause inebriation accompanied by tremors. *Chronic abuse leads to seizures and mental confusion. It can manifest interactions with anti-inflammatory drugs and cortisone.

- **Contraindications**

The toxicity of the essential oil has an amazing action characterized by an initial excitement followed by muscle paresis, inebriation and profound hypnosis; 45 drops cause hypnotic effect for 12 hours.

Helichrysum

Helichrysum essential oil is known for its soothing, antihistamine, antineuralgic, mycological, decongestant and antiasthmatic properties. The benefits are seen above all in the treatment of respiratory system disorders, such as cough, phlegm, inflammation of the mucous membranes of allergic origin. Helichrysum essential oil is indicated for both internal and external use. It is also known for its diuretic, sudorific and detoxifying properties. Its strength lies in the ability to eliminate toxic residues from tissues, especially from the kidneys and liver. It is also an excellent aid in case of slimming diets. It is also good for the skin, as it regenerates it, eliminating spots, scars, thickening and lesions. Great for lymphatic drainage massages. Helichrysum essential oil also has a strong soothing and protective action, anti free radicals, and is therefore excellent if you add a few drops to your normal sunscreen.

Furthermore, it fights gum disease and becomes an excellent natural mouthwash when added to a fresh mallow or sage-based herbal tea for rinsing. The medicinal use of this essence dates back to the dawn of herbal science, in ancient manuals it is indicated for the treatment of skin diseases. It is handed down in Greek mythology that the drops of the precious essential oil were Ariadne's recipe for happiness, abandoned by Theseus, as they helped her heal the wounds of the heart. The Helichrysum is a flower that does not wither even after being picked.

- Part used: flowers and flowering tops. If the distillation of the plant material occurs within 24 hours of harvesting, the young plants have a greater yield than the amount of oil produced by the older plants.
- Extraction method: steam distillation.
- Base note: its sunny, warm and woody scent underlines a strong attachment of this plant to the earth from which it draws its typical base note.

- **Natural detoxifier**

Just add a couple of drops of essential oil to the morning tea, before breakfast, remembering that burdock, weed, dandelion and artichoke are among the best detoxifiers; it also purifies the liver: take 1 drop a day for two weeks.

- **Environmental diffusion**

1 drop of Cajeput essential oil for each square meter of the environment in which it spreads, by means of an essential oil burner or in the water of radiator humidifiers, to purify the air and in case of flu symptoms.

- **Relaxing bath**

Mix 10 drops of helichrysum essential oil with the hot water in the tub. This bath will also have an excellent anti-aging effect on the epidermis, it will increase its tone and elasticity, making it soft and silky.

- **Purifying treatment**

To be done once a year. For four weeks, after breakfast sip a cup of herbal tea in which we will have mixed 1 teaspoon of natural honey and 1 drop of helichrysum. This treatment purifies and detoxifies our body and increases the immune system.

- **Contraindications**

It has no particular contraindications, but it is advisable to consult your doctor for any external applications in subjects taking anticoagulants; it is not recommended in pregnancy and in children. Usually it does not cause skin irritation but as with any product that is applied for the first time it is advisable to carry out a small test on a portion of the skin to evaluate any hypersensitivity to its excipients. Keep out of reach of children. Do not use during pregnancy and while breastfeeding.

Sage

Sage is particularly well known for its anti-inflammatory, balsamic, digestive and expectorant properties. It is also able to cure painful menstrual syndromes and menopausal disorders, in particular that annoying disorder called "caldane": for this reason it is also called "natural estrogen". It offers a good response against water retention, edema, rheumatism and migraines and is also indicated in gingivitis and abscesses.

It is a "deterrent" of diabetes and accelerates the healing process after an injury. In ancient times, it was considered a sacred plant. Its name derives from the Latin, salvere, from which "to save", because it is believed to be beneficial for any evil. In the Middle Ages it was customary to put a few leaves, rich in essential oil, in the mouth, before going to sleep, to encourage divining dreams or problem solving. In fact, one of the names with which sage was defined in ancient times was "clear eye".

It was supposed to strengthen vision and inward gaze: to help one "see" more clearly.

If inhaled, it induces calm and serenity in the presence of stress, nervousness, anguish, fears and paranoia. Excellent support to overcome midlife crises and menopause, for people who no longer dare, the resigned, who feel "too old" and live in a state of depression.

It acts on an emotional level, on our creativity, allowing us to express ourselves and "poetic license" worthy of born artists; instills courage to carry out creative projects or take exams. In case of depression, take 1 drop of essential oil of clary sage and 1 of peppermint in a teaspoon of honey (or a sugar cube) twice a day.

- **Balancing of the female hormonal system**

Diluted in almond oil and massaged on the body, the marked effects on the reproductive system have a beneficial effect on somatizations deriving from their imbalance, such as lymphatic stagnation, cellulite, premenstrual syndrome, menopausal hot flashes, menstrual pain, amenorrhea or abundant menstruation, alopecia due to hormonal.

- **Packs for oily skin**

Put 10-12 drops of Salvia essential oil in 200 ml of water. With cloths or gauze compresses, make long-lasting compresses on the skin of the face. Make these compresses for at least a quarter of an hour and repeat them twice a week, regularly.

- **Contraindications**

Contrary to the "officinal" variety it does not irritate, it does not sensitize and it is not toxic, but taken in high doses it causes drowsiness, paralysis and convulsions.

Sage essential oil is contraindicated in pregnancy and breastfeeding. It is not recommended to use it in conjunction with iron-based medicines or substances and not to associate it with the intake of alcoholic beverages, as it can enhance the effects of alcohol..

Angelica

The healing properties of Angelica are said to have been revealed to a monk by an angel, hence its name. Useful during the winter months, when colds and flu viruses are raging. It is said to be a fertility aid, as it helps regulate the female cycle. Strong immunostimulant useful for fighting numerous infections, especially if of a chronic nature, take 2-3 drops of angelica essence diluted in a teaspoon of mother tincture of propolis, two or three times a day. The oil promotes healing of bronchial inflammations as it dissolves phlegm and promotes expectoration. Indicated for the treatment of colitis, spastic colitis and digestive difficulties. Specific for diverticulitis.

- Effective purifying, 1 drop a day for twenty-eight days is recommended during seasonal changes. Helps recover strength in convalescence.

A complete bath with the addition of 8 drops of angelica essential oil helps stimulate sweating, thus helping the body to eliminate excess fluids and toxins.
Against travel sickness in case of nausea during travel and to counteract the feeling of tiredness, 1 drop on a handkerchief, the perfume calms the nervous system and helps regulate stomach activity. In case of anxiety, insomnia and agitation. Cast out fears and fortify. Gives energy, restores and comforts in the toughest moments.

- **Contraindications**

Angelica is always contraindicated in case of pregnancy and breastfeeding. It is also not recommended to take them when exposed to sunlight because they contain furanocoumarins, phototoxic substances.
In case of hypersensitivity to angelica, bleeding, a laxative effect and fever may also occur..

Lavender

Lavender is grown for its many applications in cosmetics, phytotherapy and aromatherapy as well as as an ornament for gardens, flower beds and borders. Originally from southern and western Europe, the Provençal one is the most famous; it was already a precious plant for the ancient Romans who put bunches of flowers in the water of the thermal baths.

The rather fragrant flowers are grouped in thin blue-violet spikes. Lavender was already used then as a base for refined perfumes and to prepare decoctions and infusions used for the beauty of skin and hair. In the more recent past we know that in every city or country house there was no wardrobe or chest of drawers that did not have sachets of lavender to perfume the linen and keep moths away.

This delicate custom is now making a comeback and reminds us of ancient traditions and sensations of cleanliness and care for the home. The French chemist, Renè Maurice Gattefossé, who is credited with the invention of the term "aromatherapy" in 1928, and who contributed to the resurgence of interest in the use of essential oils for therapeutic purposes, had at his own expense, noted that the Lavender essential oil, which he was using for perfume blends, had remarkable ability to heal burn wounds.

In fact, while he was working on perfumes he accidentally burned his arm and as a reaction he slipped it into the liquid closest to him. It so happened that that liquid was precisely lavender essential oil which made him heal from the burn in a very short time.

- Part used: flowering tops.
- Extraction method: steam distillation.
- Heart note: herbaceous scent, very sweet, slightly floral.

Lavender essential oil has both external and internal use. Combined with creams, or dropping a few drops into hot bath water, or even applied directly to the skin for massages, it helps purify fatty and impure epidermis, facilitates the healing of sores, abrasions and wounds, stimulates circulation, especially that of the scalp. The aroma emanating from lavender essential oil is relaxing and sedative and massaged on the back of the neck it seems to help keep lice away.

- **Relaxing**

If inhaled, it exerts a rebalancing action on the central nervous system, being simultaneously tonic and sedative; calms anxiety, agitation, nervousness; relieves headaches and stress-induced ailments; helps to fall asleep in case of insomnia.

A natural migraine remedy is to add 10 drops of lavender essential oil and 2 drops of peppermint essential oil to a shot glass (50 mL) of vegetable oil. Rub the temples with a circular massage using this compound.

Chronic headache sufferers can do this 2 or 3 times a day. Lavender essential oil is also a natural remedy for ear infections.

Add to 2 tablespoons of vegetable oil, 2 drops of lavender essential oil, 2 drops of eucalyptus radiata essential oil and 2 drops of tea tree. Rub and massage gently around the ears.

- **Childhood disorders**

It is an excellent essence for children: colic, irritability, colds, agitation at night, can be relieved by a massage on the neck or chest with lavender essential oil or with a few drops of the essence placed on the pillow or in the water of the radiator humidifiers.

- **Environmental diffusion**

1 drop of lavender essential oil for every square meter of the environment in which it spreads, by means of an essence burner or in the water of radiator humidifiers to relieve headaches, nervous tension, stress, insomnia.

- **Invigorating bath**

10 drops in tub water, emulsify by shaking the water vigorously, then immerse yourself for 10 minutes to take advantage of the decongestant action for the muscular system and for rheumatic and joint pain.

- **Contraindications**

Lavender essential oil has no particular contraindications. However, always remember to use it by inhalation or in friction and, if in doubt, always consult your doctor before using it. In fact, it is good to remember that essential oil, although it is considered safe, could have some contraindications if used improperly or excessively. Therefore, the consultation of the doctor or herbalist must be requested. Lavender essential oil is one of the few oils in this family that can also be used pure, although it is always recommended to dilute it in water, creams or gels.

- As with many other essential oils, pregnant or nursing women should avoid using lavender essential oil.
- It is also recommended that patients with diabetes to stay away from lavender oil.
- Some people may also experience nausea, vomiting and headaches due to using the wrong essential oil.
- Most importantly, lavender oil should never be ingested, but only applied topically or inhaled through means of aromatherapy or similar activities.
- Ingestion may cause serious health complications, characterized by blurred vision, difficulty breathing, burning eyes, vomiting and diarrhea.

Himalayan flowers for the sixth chakra

Himalayan Flower Enhancers directly affect the various energy levels controlled by the Chakras, removing negative feelings and stimulating positive ones. The Himalayan Flower Enhancers were identified by Tanmaya in 1990, during a stay of several months in a Himalayan valley. The term Enhancers means catalysts, because the essences are not only remedies aimed at working on negative emotions and inner states but also favor very deep processes of energy rebalancing and spiritual development to bring to light qualities buried within the person. They can be taken pure alone or diluted together with Bach flowers or other flowers. Tanmaya's first preparations involved nine combinations, seven directly connected to the plexuses, better known by the Indian name of chakra plus a general catalyst and a flower particularly suitable for children; subsequently their number multiplied with the discovery of new flowers, suitable for modulating specific emotions.

They are Flowers with a very rapid and powerful effect, unlike Bach Flowers, which are among the slowest and most delicate; this power is sometimes very useful, other times it can represent a risk of excessive action. While Bach Flowers can be considered primarily emotional remedies, i.e. aimed at rebalancing human emotions, Himalayan Flowers, thanks to the nature of the soil on which they grow, essentially address the spiritual dimension of man, stimulating the need for prayer, of meditation and connection with the divine that dwells in him.

Himalayan floral essences are liquid extracts that contain the energy of the flower to be administered generally orally, and can also be used in bath water, sprayed on the body or in the environment, or combined with oil for massage.

Clarity

Increases clarity, awareness, insight, perception, intuition, insight, spirituality, clairvoyance, meditation, concentration, personal power, ability to see into the heart of things and understand, the ecstasy, the sense of the Cosmic One.

Provides clarity and direction, the ability to see signs. Helps headaches, reduces excess sexual energy, helps overcome isolation, alienation, lack of meaning in life. It is helpful in lack of concentration, of self-awareness when clarity and direction are lacking. Helps with headaches, balances excess sexual energy; it also helps to overcome isolation, alienation, meaninglessness of life.

An energy blockage in the sixth Chakra can cause a dysfunction of the endocrine system with consequent pathologies that can also be serious. On a mental level this could cause a psychic block, a dissociation with one's deep self, confusion, loss of memory, clarity, difficulty in choosing and deciding. Real-world knowledge and reasoning skills are impaired. The dosage of essences, pure or diluted, is two drops under the tongue several times a day.

Californian flowers for the sixth chakra

The Californian Flowers extend the Bach Flowers.
Richard Kats and Patricia Kaminski, founders of the FES (Flower Essence Society), together with the work of other researchers have discovered more than 150 flowers since 1979. They work on more modern and current specific problems which at the time Bach lived did not they were so preponderant or they weren't talked about like today: anorexia and bulimia, sexual disorders, diseases deriving from environmental pollution. It is possible to create composite essences by combining Bach and Californian flowers, as well as essences from other flower therapy repertoires from other parts of the world. Californian flower remedies are prepared in the same simple way as Bach flowers, by placing wild flower corollas in a glass bowl filled with spring water and leaving them to infuse in the sun for a few hours. This liquid, very rich in vital force, is then filtered, diluted in brandy and used for the preparation of the so-called stock bottles (or concentrates).
The choice of essences, as with Bach flowers, is always personalized and in relation to the mood and emotions you want to rebalance. Once the remedy or remedies indicated for the personal problem have been chosen, two drops of each are poured into a small bottle with a 30 ml dropper, filled with natural mineral water and two teaspoons of brandy as a preservative.

The dosage is 4 drops 4 times a day, for a period of a few weeks or in any case until the symptoms improve or disappear.

Being a completely natural and non-toxic cure, they have no contraindications, do not cause side effects, can be combined without problems with both traditional and homeopathic medicines (of which they are considered complementary) or other flower therapy remedies.

Black Eyes Susan

For people who have experienced trauma or suffering so great that it has been removed, but which has led to states of depression, anxiety, anguish, which seem to emerge for no apparent reason. This flower helps integrate all that has been removed. It brings light into the inner darkness, promotes the elimination of emotional toxins by developing the courage to develop the dark side of the personality and stimulate awareness and the positive transformation of emotional experience.

Therefore it is useful in the case of old repressed traumas, emotional amnesia, insomnia and depression without motivation.

Once the individual Black Eyes Susan can address such buried parts of the psyche and direct them into an appropriate therapeutic environment, they will experience a strong awakening of energies.

Black Eyes Susan brings back light and awareness, helping the individual to integrate and transform unacknowledged parts of the psyche.

California Poppy

For those who are attracted to the spiritual and etheric world and resort to charismatic guides, drugs or magical rituals, allowing themselves to be dazzled. In many cases, when the individual first opens up to a larger spiritual vision, he or she is pulled in the direction of Lucifer's light. This light seems beneficial, but in reality it stuns and dazzles the person, robbing him of his inner power. Those in need of California Poppy are fascinated by spirituality or are drawn to psychic experiences outside of the self, rather than engaging in a balanced process of spiritual and moral growth.

- They may be attracted to a broad spectrum of dazzling phenomena, including drug use (especially psychedelic drugs), occult rituals, religious cults, or charismatic teachers.

California Poppy people can also be mesmerized by social glamor and notoriety, easily identify with the lives of mass media stars, and indulge in whims or ephemeral causes. Such individuals expect, "with eyes," to be able to find somewhere outside themselves the spiritual treasure they seek.

Because they do not strengthen and develop a solid inner life, they are often susceptible to techniques and influences which open the psychic faculties too quickly, especially before these energies are balanced with the energies of the heart and thought.

California Poppy stabilizes the golden light of the heart, promoting greater self-responsibility and peaceful inner growth.

In this way the individual finds the true treasure he seeks, the golden solar force of the reawakened human heart.

Filaree

For people who lack the ability to take the bigger picture of day-to-day events. They get totally involved in small things of little importance in which they get lost and which become excessive and disproportionate, often obsessive worries. These cause him to waste an enormous amount of time and psychic energy. Immeasurable concern for everyday problems. Annoying, obsessive personalities who are generally very censorious and in constant disagreement with other people's ways of doing or not doing, dressing. Excessively preoccupied with minor problems of daily life and physical ailments that limit active participation in life. They usually express their pains or sorrows, as well as reproaches. Their monotonous way of communicating makes them boring and obsessive in storytelling. They can be hypochondriacs, because they pay attention to everything.

The essence helps to broaden the vision in the daily setbacks. When well directed, these people have tremendous inner strength and reserve, which can be of great value.

They can suffer from tics, tremors and rituals of all kinds. Very fussy.

In balance, they are very strong and valuable people.

Attachment to the formal aspects of household management, allowing activities such as cleaning the house to become too important, not allowing the individual to participate in social life.

- Filaree helps these individuals make a fundamental shift in perspective, instilling a more cosmic vision, thus helping them to see the issues of everyday life in the right perspective.

Filaree, in particular, frees the too contracted psychic energy, spreading it more and making it more receptive to the influence of the spirit.

Fuchsia

For people who remove emotions such as anger, pain, sexuality, emotional shock out of fear of their intensity or due to educational and cultural conditioning and somatize them.

There is an inability to express feelings. These repressed feelings resurface in the form of hyper-emotionality. They are people who cry easily, have a heightened emotionality that hides deep emotional traumas and accuse various psychosomatic symptoms such as migraine and stomach pain.

This false emotionality or suffering acts as a cover for deeper emotions that appear too strong and heavy to integrate with the psyche. They are people who can pathologically sublimate aspects of the personality (external asceticism).

The remedy allows even the most painful and violent emotions to emerge and to be consciously faced, so that the person can express himself in a more authentic way and free himself from torment.

It produces a catharsis, the release and knowledge of stifled but deeply ingrained emotions that need to be expressed. It is the flower that connects us with our emotional "shadow".

- For sexuality that is sublimated with other psychosomatic emotions.

The Fuchsia individual learns to recognize pain and other deep feelings more immediately, thus giving the life of the soul the possibility to become emotionally authentic and vital.

Lavander

Nervousness and hyperstimulation cause tiredness and a sense of emptiness. They are people who can't pull the plug, they have physical energy that they can't discharge.
Lavander flower helps those people who excessively absorb spiritual influences. They tend to be highly aware and mentally active, with a strong attraction to spiritual practices and various forms of meditation. However they often take in much more energy than their body can actually absorb. "Tight as a string" is a typical phrase to describe this type of person.
They mostly have head problems, such as migraines, or vision problems and tension in the neck and shoulders.
They are very often afflicted with insomnia or other nervous diseases. Lavander primarily works to sedate and calm these people; at a deeper level, he teaches how to moderate and regulate psycho-spiritual energy.
In this way, the Lavander individual learns to use their highly sensitive abilities in balance with the needs of the body.

Queen Anne's Lace

Lack of inner sight, that is, of psychic perception of oneself and of the world. Lack of intuition and inner sensitivity, inability to go beyond appearances. It teaches to go beyond appearances and to look at things with a more objective eye. This flower helps remove debris from emotional perspective that distorts "clear vision." Re-harmonises the upper and lower chakras so that you stay connected to the Earth, maintaining a clear and objective vision and intuition. They are personalities who avoid seeing what they don't want, what is painful and uncomfortable for them, or what could jeopardize the story of their life.

They generally have linear, rigid and structured thinking, with little openness to new knowledge. They read the circumstances and interpret them, but not in a very fortunate way. They are not very objective, bad judges, without much criterion of reality and with a lack of common sense. They look without seeing and without registering what they see.

Queen Anne's Lace is an important remedy for this transition of consciousness. It helps remove the debris from the emotional perspective that distorts a "clear view."

Such imbalances in the "third eye" chakra, i.e. the center of clairvoyant faculties, often arise from problems in the lower chakras, when emotional and instinctual energies such as sexuality are not well integrated by the individual.

- Queen Anne's Lace brings both "higher" and "lower" energies into harmony, so that one stays in touch with the Earth, yet maintains a clear and objective vision and intuition. Queen Anne's Lace is useful for many people who seek balanced psychic openness, or who have vision problems related to an emerging clairvoyance.

The Queen Anne's Lace flower helps to keep one's feet on the ground, to purify oneself and to refine and sensitize the "clear vision" of the individual.

Australian flowers for the sixth chakra

The Australian Bush Flowers are today 69 plus 19 essences created by the combination of Australian Flowers and were introduced by Ian White, Australian biologist and psychologist. They are not yet well known and used in Italy by the general public, but they are highly appreciated by flower therapists and we find Australian flowers included in many herbal and homeopathic complexes. They are among the most powerful and widely used flowers after Bach Flowers, they have a very high energy, one of the highest among floral remedies. Australian Aborigines have always used Flowers to treat discomfort or emotional imbalances, as was the case in ancient Egypt, India, Asia and South America.

The dose, for both adults and children, consists of seven drops to be taken twice a day (morning and evening) under the tongue, or in a little water. The essences should be taken for about twenty days or a month, except for particularly powerful essences.

Being a completely natural and non-toxic cure, they have no contraindications, do not cause side effects, can be combined without problems with both traditional and homeopathic medicines (of which they are considered complementary) or other flower therapy remedies. You can prepare a single remedy (whose action will then be particularly "targeted", deep and fast), or mix different remedies together; in this case it is advisable not to exceed 4 or 5 essences and, if possible, try to choose flowers with similar and synergistic properties to treat a specific problem.

Australian flowers are also very effective when applied to the skin and can be added to creams, gels, massage oils, medicated ointments or diluted in bath water. For a topical treatment, the recommended quantity is about 7 drops of each chosen remedy, to be mixed in half a cup of cream; instead, 15–20 drops of each essence should be poured into the bathtub.

The duration of treatment always depends on the individual response. A positive reaction is often obtained in about two weeks and on average two months are sufficient to rebalance numerous psychophysical problems. Some particularly "powerful" flowers (such as, for example, Waratah) usually exert a very rapid action, even in a few days. Many times, after resolving an inner discomfort or conflict, other emotional imbalances can emerge, which will gradually be treated with the corresponding flowers.

Bush Fuchsia

Important remedy in learning problems.

It allows the integration of both cerebral hemispheres, solving the majority of learning problems that come from imbalances between the two hemispheres (dyslexia, stuttering, difficulty in articulating oral language, aphasia). It helps in having confidence in public speaking. Inability to balance the logical and rational side with the intuitive and creative side.

Inability to perceive or follow instincts.

Useful in cases of inability to study for long periods without losing concentration. By balancing the two cerebral hemispheres, it helps to get in touch with your intuitions. It helps to find the ability to distinguish and interpret information and perceptions. It helps develop intuition and trust your instincts.

For those who spend a lot of time in front of video terminals or other electronic devices and feel a little dull at the end of the day. This flower increases clarity of language and communication and gives the confidence needed to speak in public.

Increases the ability to concentrate and therefore to understand a text or study material. It increases the desire to read in children and also increases their confidence and security in the classroom and in front of exams.

As it stimulates the development of logical and rational functions (left cerebral hemisphere), it will also do so with the creative and intuitive aspects, corresponding to the right cerebral hemisphere.

It allows to balance the functions of both hemispheres when there is an excessive predominance of one over the other. Another aspect of this essence is its ability to facilitate movement coordination. Another property, related to verbal expression, is that it helps in conversation by improving the tone, inflection and melody of the voice. It also improves hearing ability, especially in cases of chronic infections. Useful in rebalancing the hypothalamus following prolonged use of contraceptive pills or hormone replacement treatment.

Excellent for tuning in to one's intuition, for hand-eye coordination and the ability to express ideas, it allows people to believe in their intuition and their own way of acting, rather than doing what others say. In the case of dyslexia, it is necessary to take Bush Fuchsia for 15 consecutive days and repeat the treatment after a break of a couple of weeks. It is the essence of choice of the pituitary.

Excellent for ear infections, vertigo, labyrinthitis and nausea.

Yellow Cowslip Orchid

They are people who direct their energies above all to the intellect, so much so that they often block their feelings. This imbalance leads to criticizing and judging and being extremely bureaucratic and skeptical and exaggeratedly cautious in accepting things. It is the flower connected to the pituitary gland.
Balances the pituitary especially for women who have been on the pill for many years.
Gives interest in the problems of others.
Develop impartiality, the ability to recognize details and objectivity in general analysis, open-mindedness, ability to quickly understand concepts. These personalities are overly rational and analytical.
For them the most important thing is the intellect; the rest is secondary and therefore does not justify any concern. They are obsessive, scrupulous and stuck on little things. They are fond of rules and order, they observe other people, critically. They are skeptical, irritable, suspicious and cautious; they don't like confrontation, but prefer to distance themselves.
They are naturally sociable, charismatic, and know how to quickly understand the needs of others.
They must learn to accept ideas and people without criticism. Their emotional world is colored with irritability, meanness, irony, partiality, bad mood, irascibility, coldness, acidity, detachment and caution in dialogue.

Bach flowers for the sixth chakra

Bach flowers are an alternative medicine created by the British doctor Edward Bach, born on 24 September 1886 in Moseley from a Welsh family in England. He graduated in medicine in 1912 and immediately worked in the emergency room of the university hospital where he began to be noticed for the large amount of time he devoted to patients. He was immediately critical of other doctors, who studied the disease as if it were separate from the individual, without focusing on the patients themselves.

It is well known that our emotional states have a profound influence on our well-being and health. An altered emotional state that repeats itself every day creates real dysfunctions in our body.

Ninety per cent of the causes of human disease come from planes beyond the physical, and it is on these planes that symptoms begin to manifest before the physical body shows any disturbance. If we can identify the negative moods that crop up when we get sick, we can fight the disease better and heal faster. Using floral remedies you try to influence the deeper structures from which the disease originates. Bach flowers rebalance the emotions. They address only and exclusively how we react emotionally to the vicissitudes, experiences and problems in our days. They give great serenity and peace, courage or strength, they help us feel at the fullest of our possibilities.

They can be useful in the face of an illness, not from a physical point of view but just as a mood support. The person is seen as a complete individual where emotions are a pivotal point, and not just as a physical body with symptoms. It is therefore necessary to analyze the emotional state and not the physical symptoms, based on this the suitable remedies are found. In fact subjects with identical physical problems react and live with different emotions and feelings. Bach flowers have no contraindications and do not interact with medicines.

Bach has thus divided the 38 flowers from which the remedies are drawn. The very first flowers discovered by Bach were the so-called "12 Healers", which the Welsh doctor promptly began to experiment first on himself and then on his patients; the other 26 were discovered a short time later, divided into "7 Helpers" and "19 Assistants".

Dr Bach later abandoned the distinction between 'Healers', 'Helpers' and 'Assistants' as superfluous, but many people around the world still use it. Bach Flowers do not help to repress negative attitudes, but transform them into their positive side. The Bach Flowers associated with the first chakra are only in general, because the flowers must still be chosen based on the emotion that is not in harmony and must be balanced.

Beech

It belongs to the category of "Assistants".
Who needs this flower is an intolerant and hypercritical person, can't find anything good in his life, moreover he notices defects in everything and everyone; his observation ability is above the norm finding negativity in everything around him, nothing escapes him.
This attitude is manifested more openly in the family sphere, with friends and colleagues. The person with this disposition will often speak his mind about him, but in a polite way, he will always find a flaw to fix; endowed with a great spirit of observation that he could use in the world of work, she will be trusted for his sincerity.
The flower remedy calms the desire to criticize and increases the level of tolerance. The positive aspect of Beech is well represented in the literary or film critic but also in the analyst or therapist. In this case the Beech person puts his strong analytical and critical characteristics at the service of others. Negatively, he only runs the risk of not accepting anything of the differences of others.
With Beech you accept the points of view and tastes of others with ease and understanding.
This Flower is also indispensable for people who experience food allergies and intolerances, because it helps them to express their thoughts and therefore not to tolerate everything and everyone.

It is also advisable for all those unbearable situations such as excessive heat.

Beech-related moods and symptoms in order of importance:

- Intolerance
- The faults of others are easily seen
- Annoyance about anything
- Prejudices
- No can be tolerated
- Inflexible with others
- Intolerance
- Authoritarianism with intolerance
- Exaggerated anger at the cause
- Intolerance with arrogance
- Excessive attention to detail.

To prepare the floral remedy, take some twigs of about 15 cm with their flowers and fill a pot 3/4 full, then boil for half an hour.

Chicory

It belongs to the category of "Healers".
Whoever needs this flower is a person who dedicates his mental and physical strength to the needs of the people he loves, exercising a certain amount of control. Usually the person with this nature is easily recognized because he always has something to fix for the loved one: such as the collar of the shirt, the hair, the make-up, he also gives advice on clothing, on the partner, on friendships, and asks that it be reciprocated , as if it were a job, an assembly line I give to you, you give to me. You love others, but you want to be reciprocated.
Classic interested manipulator character who probably won't easily accept this definition. But if it often comes to mind: after everything I've done, he looks at how he treats me. Then it's time to consider Chicory. The person with this disposition will always think how to improve the life of the people he loves, because he wants them to be happy, but the flower remedy will help them understand that everyone has their own destiny to follow and that it is not necessary to manipulate; furthermore he will learn to give love, without expecting anything in return. With Chicory you understand the true qualities of love.
You give protection and security to others in complete autonomy.
Chicory related moods and symptoms in order of importance:

- Pride in your home
- Jealousy and possessiveness with those you love
- Possessiveness with a need to manipulate others
- Jealousy with possessiveness
- Easy crying
- Exaggerated love for the house
- Hypochondriasis to get attention
- Critical meddling in other people's affairs
- Sense of abandonment in parents when their children become Depressed from not being loved
- Need for recognition
- Greed as greed
- Desire to command with authoritarianism
- Abandonment, for parents who recriminate when their children go their own way
- Need for order in model housewives
- Love as possessiveness towards others.

It is prepared with the sun method, and since the flower withers quickly you need to have a bowl of water ready.

Rock Water

It belongs to the "Aid" category.

Whoever needs this flower is a very strict person in his way of life, he denies himself many entertainments and pleasures in life, respecting hard and strict rules. He thinks above all about health, he wants to be strong, active, and does everything to stay that way, he wants to be a good example for others.

He is the fanatic of himself, he does not indulge in pleasures and adheres to his ideals with strength, determination and above all rigidity.

Unlike the fanatic who wants to convince others (Vervain), Rock Water claims to be perfect and an example for others. Sometimes this mental rigidity has its physical counterparts. The ideals of reference can be different and range from sport, to nutrition, to work.

The Rock Water remedy doesn't stop people from having high ideals and trying to reach them, but it helps to limit excesses, have more flexibility and not be so intransigent with themselves. Rock Water is the only Bach remedy that is not a flower, but pure spring water.

With Rock Water life becomes adaptation, one's conceptions and ideals are lived with freedom and kindness

Rock Water related moods and symptoms in order of importance:

- Pride that makes us masters of ourselves
- Need for perfection

- Inflexible with themselves
- Severity towards oneself
- Perfection is sought
- Dogmatic idealism
- Self-satisfaction.

Vervain

It belongs to the category of "Healers".

Who needs this flower is a person who combines his psychic and physical forces to convince others of his ideas, his ideals, transforming himself into true missionaries, inflexible and intolerant. One is easily enthusiastic and absolutely wants to convince others of one's opinions as well. Injustices infuriate, taking sides. The fanatic, the enthusiastic driver, the champion of justice. Vervain has a constant need to feel alive by fighting battles and involving others in his missions. The excessive state of Vervain makes at times fanatical, hyperactive and tense.

The remedy is given to help such people stop from time to time so that body and mind can regenerate. Vervain leads to stillness in taking pleasure in life and the passage of time instead of always feeling the need to be active.

With Vervain you live life with enthusiasm, with respect for others. He is a passionate inspirer and open to change.

Vervain-related moods and symptoms in order of importance:

- Need to convince others
- You want to convince others
- Idealism and fanaticism
- Need to always be engaged in some battle
- Tension

- Excessive self-esteem in which one thinks one is always right
- Aggression due to impulsivity
- Bulimia with voracity
- Hyperactivity.

Vine

It belongs to the "Aid" category.

Who needs this flower is a person who wants to command everyone: he is a boss, a leader, a tyrant. In life he can't stand being commanded but, on the contrary, he loves to command; he is always in charge of something, of a company, of a team, of a group, of the family, he makes decisions for everyone because he is certain that he is doing their good.

Leader and dictator, what a huge difference. These two figures are the positive and negative representation of Vine. In the blocked phase Vine wants to convince others by dominating them, deciding for them. Vine people often have important roles in their work and in their interests and in the transformed state they can be excellent leaders by inciting and guiding others without forcing them and above all with respect for others.

They are very different from Vervain-type people who instead try to convert others to their way of thinking, whereas Vine-types impose orders and discipline without admitting counteraction.

The remedy develops this positive side of the Vine personality.

With Vine, one's authority is lived with confidence in oneself and in others. You also know how to delegate to others, thus also evaluating the potential of others.

Vine-related moods and symptoms in order of importance:

- Inflexible with others
- Aggression to impose one's opinion
- Desire for command
- Tendency to dominate
- Authoritarianism by which one commands
- Intransigence
- Uncertainty that makes you arrogant.

Crab Apple

It belongs to the category of "Assistants".

Whoever needs this flower is a person who believes that he is not completely clean, as if he wanted to drive some poison out of his body, an evil that has now been generated, or that he thinks he has. One has the feeling of being dirty polluted, both physically and psychologically.

Also suitable for all those who do not accept themselves.

It is definitely the flower that has the greatest impact on the external shape, therefore on the skin and on our relationship with the body and appearance. With Crab Apple it's easier to accept yourself for who you are, valuing our positive aspects more without remaining anchored to just the physical aspect. Also useful when obsessed with cleanliness. Given its relationship with the skin, it becomes part of the Rescue Cream. The person with this disposition will accept himself more willingly; the floral remedy helps to alleviate the phobias concerning dirt and contact with things that do not belong to your home environment such as going to public toilets, the fear that you may endanger your health will vanish and you will be able to stay in contact even with apparently unclean people.

It can be applied in the form of a cream on pimples, blisters, eczema, basically any rash.

Crab Apple related moods and symptoms in order of importance:

- Excessive care of cleanliness both personal and of the house
- Lack of self-confidence in physical appearance
- Obsession with dirt
- You think you are disliked because of small physical imperfections
- Need to wash constantly
- Hypersensitive to the possibility of contagion
- Fear of contagion and of being contaminated
- Pimples and acne that make us uncomfortable
- Fear of spoiled food
- Shame
- Purification and cleaning

In flower therapy the flower is gathered in tufts together with their small branch using very sharp scissors (shears). The boiling method is used.

Number of the fifth chakra

2 is the number of the sixth chakra.

The 2 is the number of the first polarization.

Here the two initial, virtual terms are represented coexisting, sun and moon, and in the act of reuniting: the lingam that literally penetrates the apex of the triangle, the yoni, as if to generate.

What is generated by 2 is first of all 3, a principle still unmanifest, but the basis and creator of all things. In this regard, the Tao-te-ching confirms: «One produced 2, 2 produced 3, 3 produced all numbers», therefore 2 is the symbol of all the dualities for which we exist, so heaven and earth are the polarization of primordial unity, the process of cosmic manifestation involving the separation into two halves of the world egg.

«I am one that becomes two» reiterates an ancient Egyptian inscription, and nothing is actually conceivable without immediately conceiving its opposite: two is masculine and feminine, light and dark, manifest and unmanifest, mortal and immortal. , me and self, black and white, good and bad. Yin and yang are the perfect symbolism, even graphic, of this duality implicit in existence. It is impossible to eliminate the duality of thought because, precisely because of this duality, it exists. The 2 therefore expresses the archetype of all existing complementarities.

It is therefore the symbol of all dualities, that is of all that is present or can be present in the cosmos-microcosm.

In this sense, therefore, here resides the power that oversees and directs the possibility of any manifestation or non-manifestation of body and mind, matter and spirit. It is the center that gives the go, the absolute potentiality, as its name itself says, ajna, "center of command". Furthermore, ajna, containing the germ of all dualities, is also implicitly the possibility of knowing them a priori, having them in oneself as a direct acquisition, even before they manifest themselves; that is, in full, the possibility of foresight, as on the other hand another name that is attributed to it seems to confirm: "third eye". The downward pointing triangle here is undoubtedly a symbol of the feminine or will directed towards manifestation, penetrated by the masculine lingam, or will directed towards the unmanifest. The two images constitute, in turn, one of the most present symbols in the human imagination of duality which, fertilising, gives rise to the three and therefore «the thousand beings».

- In the positive valence, Two can be considered feminine, intuitive and corresponds to the protective instinct.
- In negative valence, Two can be greedy, suffocating and frustrating. The frustrating aspect has come from the disappointment and dissatisfaction of the human spirit which is always denied the first position.

The number Two characterized by the archetype the Child is associated with the tenderness of the mother, he could exchange the love of a couple with the need for someone close to lean on and trust because he loves being able to do everything together in always being together with the desire to live in total peace.

He will always be a tender inner child with a need for nourishment through the pleasure of being in a couple with his own family, rooted in the stability of the union.

The tenderness of the archetype related to the number Two impresses nostalgia for a lost paradise when confronted with the pain of the world, when he lacks a loved one in facing the reality of life he risks losing contact with divinity; at this point he realizes that unfortunately evil also exists, he is often injured on the emotional level and thus needs someone to protect him by holding him tightly, he must feel contained in the arms of those who love him, to feel comforted and possibly at peace center of attention, he fears suffering a lot with the fear that everything will fall on him.

Phisical exercises

- **Exercise 1**

Do some relaxation exercises by shaking your arms and legs.
Sit on the floor with your back straight and then do alternate breathing for a few minutes.

- **Exercise 2**

Assume the quadruped position and perform the "horse's back / cat's arched back" exercise 7 times.

- **Exercise 3**

Starting sitting on your heels, slowly lower your torso forward until your forehead touches the floor.
The arms are extended beside the body with palms facing up.
Breathe deeply a few times focusing on your forehead, then slowly lift your torso vertebra by vertebra until your back is straight.
Place your hands on the back of your neck to gently support your head, open your eyes and look up for a few seconds.
Repeat the exercise 3 more times.

- **Exercise 4**

When seated, assume the following position: the middle fingers, stretched out, are facing forward and touch each other as well as the tips of the thumbs, which however are directed towards the chest.
The other fingers will be bent and will make the second phalanges meet successively.
Inhale and pronounce the mantra "ksham" repeatedly while exhaling, repeating the exercise 7 times.

- **Exercise 5**

Lie on your back, close your eyes and relax.
Place the palm of the left hand on the center of the forehead and the right on top of it (the position of the hand should naturally follow the line of the forearms).
Keep your hands resting gently on your forehead for a few minutes, then imagine blue energy entering your chakra and flooding your body as you exhale.
Continue like this for at least 5 minutes, then place your hands on your sides, palms on the ground and stay like this, relaxing a little longer.

Stones for the 6th Chakra

In crystallotherapy stones of the 6th Chakra are considered those of indigo or purple color, of any type of brightness or transparency.

- The placement zone of the stones is the forehead region.
- Crystals that can balance the sixth chakra are: amethyst, fluorite, sapphire, boulder opal, moonstone, sugillite, tanzanite, lepidolite, cat's eye.
- The most representative base frequency stone is Amethyst.
- The most representative advanced frequency stone is Sugellite (or Luvolite).

Feel its energy passing through the sacral chakra as you hold it in your hand or wear it by ring or necklace. You don't have to buy them all, just choose the stones you prefer or which you already have.
The range of indigo/purple minerals:

- They act on the sensory organs
- Relieve headaches
- Help in case of hysteria, melancholy and epilepsy
- Facilitate access to spirituality
- Relax stressed people.

Amethyst

The term amethyst derives from the Greek word amethystos, which means "not intoxicated" and is present in various ways and uses in almost all religious practices in the world.
Amethyst is widely used to open the spiritual and psychic energy centers and this makes it one of the most important power stones.
Amethyst symbolizes compassion, humility, sincerity and spiritual wisdom. Known as the "Spirit Stone" or "Stone of Integrity", amethyst is also the Buddha stone and in Tibet it is frequently used for making rosaries called Malas which are then used in the practice of meditation.
Amethyst gives common sense and flexibility in decisions. Strengthens and improves psychic, intuitive and clairvoyant abilities by being energetically directly connected with the energy of our mind. An excellent detoxifying stone, amethyst helps with addictions and calms the nervous system by promoting the transmission of signals within it. Amethyst is an energy transmuter, it helps open doors into intense and transformative spiritual experiences. Excellent stone for the Third Eye chakra and the Crown chakra.

- One of its peculiarities is to purify other stones; in fact, amethyst is recommended to be used in combination with other stones or crystals.

Amethyst is also used in ancient traditional Chinese medicine, which prescribes the stone to relieve stomach pains or to have a peaceful sleep and not have bad dreams. Amethyst awakens one's spiritual awareness by increasing knowledge of a reality beyond matter. It helps to perceive the spiritual aspect behind the events. Thus, the Amethyst manages to be a good remedy for reworking a mourning and the consequent pain due to the loss of the loved one. It also increases the sense of justice, humility and honesty. It reduces the selfish instinct and strengthens the ability to love.

- It is an effective calmer for the mind, which promotes concentration and calms confused thoughts. It has the ability to relieve feelings of guilt, strengthening self-confidence and decreasing inferiority complexes. Its influence on the emotional sphere is expressed by helping to calm the emotionality, favoring greater clarity.

Diminish the sadness that may come in difficult times. It is an effective remedy against insomnia and nightmares so as to promote deep rest. The result is the reduction of tensions with the consequent reduction of migraines. Helps relieve swelling and bruising. Useful for solving some pathologies of the skin, lungs and nervous system.

The dark variety mitigates hypertension and stiffness and is an excellent regulator of bacterial flora.

Possible elixirs with this stone have a mild effect but all methods of preparation are possible. Works in great synergy with Bach Flowers, especially with the Agrimony remedy.

Amethyst is an excellent remedy for rebalancing the energy of environments, especially bedrooms and rooms where we welcome people who do not belong to our family.

They are also used in medical offices such as, for example, psychologists, where many people come to vent by talking about their problems and therefore the environment is affected by negative energies that must be driven away.

The zodiac signs associated with this stone are Sagittarius, Capricorn and Pisces while the corresponding Chakra is the 6th or the Third Eye.

Fluorite

The Fluorite stone owes its name to the Latin word "fluere" which means to melt, given its use as a flux in metallurgy.
The word "fluorescent" also comes from the word Fluorite as its crystals were the first fluorescent specimens to be studied.
Ancient Egyptians used Fluorite to carve statues and beetles and since Roman times, Fluorite has been used to make vases and other ornamental objects. The Chinese have used Fluorite in sacred sculptures for over 300 years. In the eighteenth century, Fluorite was pulverized in water to relieve the symptoms of kidney disease. In different parts of the world Fluorite was thought to be the "home of the rainbow" due to the mixed colors present in it. Fluorite can help increase focus and intuition. It can implement to remain impartial when the decisions must not involve us emotionally.

- Fluorite stone is highly protective and functions as an energy stabilizer. It absorbs negative energies from the environment and is effective for our Aura and Chakra cleaning.

It helps grasp higher concepts, it's a terrific stone for college students and researchers who need to analyze data and come to conclusions.

Excellent stone for strengthening bones, teeth and improving pain associated with arthritis.

- Fluorite helps revive sexual appetite.

The properties of Fluorite make it possible to protect wellness operators or anyone who is in close contact with many people from psychic manipulation, voluntary or otherwise.

In particular, it allows for innovation and inventiveness, being a very effective stone to use for mental creativity and for creating wealth and prosperity.

Fluorite works excellently with all stones, especially agate and carnelian.

Sapphire

Sapphire, in all its celestial hues, is a stone of wisdom, kingship, prophecy, and divine favor. Often used as a talisman, crystal has always been chosen to preserve purity, to detect fraud and betrayal, to protect the wearer. And it is still a noble stone of learning, mental acuity, psychic activation, and spiritual seeking.

- Its blue color brings order and healing to the mind, giving strength and alertness, as well as the ability to see beyond superficial appearances, using deeper knowledge. Stimulates the throat and third eye chakras, allowing access to deeper levels of consciousness in order to gain greater self-understanding.

Associated with the planet Saturn, in crystal therapy it improves self-discipline and helps to materialize the goals that have been set.

Blue is considered the primary color of sapphire, although it can actually be found in many other shades. The name "sapphire" derives from the Latin "sapphirus", from the Greek "sappheiros" and from the Sanskrit "sanipryam", which means precisely blue stone. It is thought that the current lapis lazuli in the past were referred to as sapphires.

However all sapphires are stones of wisdom, individual colors add different shades to it.

- Black Sapphire: leads to trust in one's intuition and wisdom.
- It protects, relieves anxiety and pain and is a useful talisman when looking for work.
- Green Sapphire: brings wisdom, fidelity and integrity. Encourage compassion for others, improve dream recall.
- Orange sapphire or Padparadscha: stimulates the desire to speak to the world directly from one's heart. It combines creativity and spirituality: it is no coincidence that it is a useful talisman for artists, writers and singers.
- Pink Sapphire: Nurtures the wisdom of resilience. Stimulates emotions and promotes love, forgiveness and forgetting the past. Increase acceptance and strength of feelings.
- Violet Sapphire: Strengthens the wisdom of spiritual awakening. Stimulates meditation, vibrates with the crown chakra and allows the Kundalini to rise unhindered. Promotes unity and peace.
- White sapphire: brings wisdom and fortitude, helping to find within oneself the best solution to overcome the difficult obstacles encountered on one's spiritual journey. It gives the mind great clarity and improves communication with the Higher Self.
- Yellow Sapphire: brings wisdom and prosperity. In addition to an increase in economic revenues, it aspires to a greater willingness to create new

solutions that make ambitions and objectives achieved.

Sapphire is great for calming the mind, aiding in the release of tension from unwanted thoughts. It encourages intuition, bringing lightness, joy and balance. Blue sapphire is very useful for spiritual growth and for increasing self-discipline, especially in daily activities that require attention.

Furthermore, it gives a lot of professional support, stimulates ingenuity and wisdom and increases common sense in carrying out one's profession. It is a stone symbol of integrity, so it is very effective for the quick and positive resolution of legal issues or in some way related to justice.

Blue sapphire, again, is a stone of love, commitment and fidelity, so much so that it can be used in engagement rings.

Boulder opal

Boulder opal is an excellent stone for progress, expansion and personal development. It helps connect our conscious with the subconscious, allowing for compensation and understanding of oneself on a psychic and mental level.

Boulder opal facilitates communication between our earthly dimension and that of other worlds of different dimensions.

Precisely because of its deep connection with the earth, it becomes an excellent ally for our roots, especially during periods of substantial changes in our lives. Allowing for emotional and mental balance, it soothes the inner soul and cleanses and brightens the personal aura, stimulating centering. It is used to access higher spirit guides and animal guides.

It can be used to stabilize personal energy. Boulder opal is excellent stone for the eyes and in communication of all verbal forms. It is an emotional balancer that aids inner beauty and fidelity.

Wearing, touching and meditating with boulder opal helps to increase mental abilities such as creative visualization, intuition and clairvoyance, untapped potentials of the mind.

Boulder opal strengthens the will to live life to the fullest.

Moonstone

Moonstone has been used for centuries in a variety of cultures. Being a perfect expression of yin energy, i.e. the mysterious and placid energy of the moon, this stone is in turn the bearer of calm, peace and balance.
The serenity and tranquility that the mineral generates has a sensual and extraordinary effect, infusing creativity and optimism with its soft glow.
Anciently, but still today, moonstone is considered a sacred stone in India.
Associated with the moon, the stone was worn by the goddess Diana and in the East moonstone amulets were often hung on fruit trees to ensure fertile and abundant crops and in the Middle Ages, by alchemists, it was believed that if held in the mouth, the stone di luna could help make appropriate decisions. Moonstone is a gem of intuition and deep understanding, it helps balance the emotional body by accentuating freedom of expression and particularly attenuates aggressive tendencies.
By bringing feminine energy, moonstone opens up our more yin side, can stimulate pineal gland functioning, balance internal hormonal cycles with the rhythms of nature, relieve menstrual and pregnancy pain, promote fertility and help stimulate the lymphatic and immune system. It can reduce swelling and excess body fluid.

- Although often considered a women's stone, moonstone can be very helpful to men in opening up their emotional self.

The finest moonstone is mainly mined from Sri Lanka. It helps to be more aware that all things are part of a cycle of constant change. The ideal and most resonant time to use moonstone is during the full moon phase. Thanks to its association with water, it appears to be very protective of people who live near seaside places. Moonstone connects the second and sixth chakras beautifully to each other, enhancing intuitive sensitivity through behaviors that are less overwhelmed by personal feelings.

- Works wonders when paired with garnet, (revealing the truth behind our illusions) and when used in conjunction with amethyst in the higher chakras.

Moonstone is a very personal gem: it reflects the soul of the person who owns it. It does not take away or add anything to the personality, but shows it as it really is: this is why it is useful during meditation. It is excellent for women, but can be indicated to men to encourage them to express their emotions. The gem is therefore used to stimulate the functioning of the pineal gland and the balance of internal hormonal cycles, adapting them to the rhythms of nature

In feng shui, moonstone is used for its calming properties, its yin energy and the fact that it recalls the element of water.

A home or office with too much yang energy can benefit from the compensation that the stone will be able to generate.

Make sure you take the best care of your moonstone, whether it's spheres and ovals, or jewelry. Clean it often and gently, trying to preserve it from exposure to strong sunlight.

As you can easily guess, unlike other crystals and other stones, the best way to recharge the stone is by exposing it to moonlight. You can choose the fresh energy of the new moon or the powerful vibrations of the full one: by taking care of your gem, you will receive abundance, energy and balance in return.

Sugillite

Sugillite owes its name to the Japanese geologist who discovered the first specimens, Ken-ichi Sugi. It is a particular stone, considered one of the stones of love and one of the most important for the fourth chakra. It represents spiritual love and wisdom, and is capable of aligning all chakras allowing the Kundalini energy to be opened and directed throughout the body.
Wearing or carrying Sugilite with you increases the search for freedom, drawing inspiration and trust. Excellent for movement disorders and epilepsy.

- Sugillite is a stone widely used to recall visions and to stimulate our third eye, allowing visionary experience and higher perceptions.

It is a stone that favors rest and inner calm. It brings us to balance left brain function and helps anyone integrate into the world or a new environment. Together with the amethyst, it amplifies the protective power of our aura.

Tanzanite

Tanzanite is a mineral, more precisely a variety of Zoisite, it was discovered in early January 1967 in northern Tanzania at the foot of the Merelani mountains near the Merelani Hills near the city of Arusha, it was enthusiastically celebrated and called as "The gem of the 20th century". The blue of the tanzanite is gorgeous and spectacular, ranging from ultramarine to a slight purplish blue/purple, the most sought after color is a blue that shows a shimmering purplish hue around it, which is extremely spectacular. Its color varies from deep blue to purple, passing through indigo.
It clarifies the mission of one's existence, allowing a greater sense of orientation with which to direct one's choices. It facilitates situations in which the mind and psychic abilities are activated and guided by the wisdom of the heart. It helps to overcome the inner crises due to the feeling of drifting, clarifying which destination to reach and overcoming the fear of wasting one's life.
Stimulates clear and pragmatic thoughts and increases self-confidence. It supports the activity of the kidneys, strengthens the nervous system, tones the tissues and replenishes body fluids.
The energetic peculiarity of tanzanite consists in its great ability to put the heart in contact with both intuitive and rational thought: the wisdom of the heart

therefore guides thought and instinct towards the right direction to follow.

It is a very suitable stone for moments of inner crisis, also because it increases self-confidence. The properties of this crystal are truly amazing. When the eye rests on Tanzanite stones of good quality and color, one feels stirred by their beauty, and the "beauty" one appreciates about them is a reflection of the mental and emotional qualities that these stones awaken in one's self.

- Due to its intrinsic characteristics, it finds splendid resonance with all the high Chakras, i.e. with the Cardiac Chakra, the Throat Chakra, the Third Eye and clearly with the Crown. The integration of mind and heart offered by Tanzanite occurs through the heart and third eye chakras.

The importance of this attunement to one's spiritual life cannot be overemphasised. The need to bring the heart into cooperation and communion with the mind is in part what is meant by the quest for wholeness. Through the Tanzanite it can create a vibrational circuit between the two chakras which is perceived as a fluctuating frequency of joy and pleasure. When the mind understands what the heart can offer it releases its pleasure to the heart which releases greater joy which causes the mind to reflect greater pleasure and the process continues. Another effect of Tanzanite integration is achieved on the throat chakra.

Under the effect of Tanzanite it is easier to express the truth of the heart with all the resources that the mind can offer. Tanzanite makes it difficult to hide or disavow what one knows from the heart.

113

Cat's eye

Cat's Eye Stone is an excellent earth grounding stone that provides very high vibrational energy and effective etheric protection due to its ability to dissipate non-harmonic energies from our aura. Cat's Eye works by amplifying the energies of other crystals, stimulating intuition and enhancing awareness, through increased creativity and kindness. Greatly increases psychic abilities and the manifestation of material things.

The cat's eye has always been believed, by mystics and esotericists, capable of giving deep philosophical thought and the ability to be wise.

It can be useful when greater concentration is needed or to stimulate healing.

Traditionally believed to protect the wearer from evil spirits.

Excellent stone for eye disorders, to improve night vision and to relieve headaches. It is also a mood regulator and is beneficial for eliminating tiredness and irritability.

The cat's eye stone is believed to protect and multiply the wearer's wealth.

For this purpose it is recommended to keep it in the same place where the money is kept.